499
499

D1528064

ON ORDER AND THINGS

ESSENTIAL POETS SERIES 115

Canadä

ONTARIO ARTS COUNCIL
CONSEIL DES ARTS DE L'ONTARIO

Guernica Editions Inc. acknowledges the support of
The Canada Council for the Arts.
Guernica Editions Inc. acknowledges the support of
the Ontario Arts Council.
Guernica Editions Inc. acknowledges the financial support of
the Government of Canada through the Book Publishing Industry Development
Program (BPIDP).
Guernica Editions Inc. acknowledges the Government of Ontario through the Ontario
Media Development Corporation's Ontario Book Initiative.

STEFAN PSENAK

ON ORDER AND THINGS

TRANSLATED BY ANTONIO D'ALFONSO

GUERNICA

TORONTO·BUFFALO·CHICAGO·LANCASTER (U.K.)

2003

Original title: *Du chaos et de l'ordre des choses*.
Published by Le Nordir, 1998.

A special thanks to Jennifer Dale, Daniel Sloate, Halli Villegas and Elana Wolff
for their precious editorial suggestions.

Guernica Editions Inc.
P.O. Box 117, Station P, Toronto (ON), Canada M5S 2S6
2250 Military Road, Tonawanda, N.Y. 14150-6000 U.S.A.

Distributors:
University of Toronto Press Distribution,
5201 Dufferin Street, Toronto, (ON), Canada M3H 5T8

Gazelle Book Services, Falcon House, Queen Square, Lancaster LA1 1RN U.K.

Independent Publishers Group,
814 N. Franklin Street, Chicago, Il. 60610 U.S.A.

First edition.
Printed in Canada.
Legal Deposit – First Quarter
National Library of Canada
Library of Congress Catalog Card Number: 20023101163.
National Library of Canada Cataloguing in Publication
Psenak, Stefan
[Du chaos et de l'ordre des choses. English]
On order and things / Stefan Psenak ; Antonio D'Alfonso, translator.
(Essential poets series ; 115)
Translation of: Du chaos et de l'ordre des choses.
ISBN 1-55071-155-5
I. D'Alfonso, Antonio. II. Title.
III. Title: Du chaos et de l'ordre des choses. English. IV. Series.
PS8581.S45D813 2003   C841'.54   C2003-900747-2
PQ3919.2.P83D813 2003

ON ORDER AND THINGS

For Sylvie and Pierre-Paul

You run with the clouds and sleep when the shadows do.

Daniel Sloate,
A Taste of Earth, A Taste of Flame

She tumbles all the way down the twenty-five stairs she had by painstakingly managed to climb, using her shadow as support. Her blouse comes undone, revealing her breasts. He stands at the top of the staircase, studying the way she turns her eyes up to him, eyes at once immensely soft, immensely wild, eyes that ask nothing in return. Her mascara is smudged. He goes down and helps her to her feet, boorishly pulling her by the arms, as he hollers in her face that she's a bitch. Unburdened, calmed, he presses her beautiful body against his. She is as cold as a corpse. Syringes filled with hope have turned her arms into rubber. He comforts her by whispering how he could love her if only she would let herself be loved. She tells him he is wrong, that there's no such thing as hope, that hope is a luxury too costly to be purchased. Who in the world really gives a damn? She needs something to drink. He offers her a cigarette. Smoke is a stage prop for dreams they'll stub out.

Later, there is pain. There is hurting all over. The fog lifts, and the mind begins to link what it did not understand to what the body experienced. Euphoria is beyond reach. Too distant. She says that the poetry in her is hurting. When she vomits, she throws up her hatred for the world. He runs his fingers through her sticky hair and splashes water on the back of her neck. When her guts start to wrench, she foolishly holds her breath. His back is assailed by cold shivers at the thought that it is he who is being asked to ward off the misfortune she has cast on herself. Again he lets a tear die on his unshaven cheeks.

Now he craves for her madly, he who becomes gentle as she makes her way out from the bottom of the night. He asks little from her, not even an explanation. He finds her beautiful, though sickness is ripping her stomach apart. He could sink his penis into her sex or mouth and hope the sperm could wash away sin. At times, he even masturbates, while watching her sleep.

She sips the bitter coffee, her eyes at once an affront and protection. She lowers her head, finding him neither handsome nor fascinating. She doesn't even like him, but enjoys certain aspects of him, such as the comforting way he says: "Wait, let me make you a cup of good coffee."

Then, one day, he buys her paper and a typewriter. She tells him it's not her birthday. He smiles. The following day, he brings her artist's gear: brushes, a large roll of canvas and a dozen cans of acrylic paint in every colour. She takes him in her arms and he feels that this time it's for real. This makes him happy because he knows she is sincere at this moment. Never will she frighten him as she did before. When they make love, she is unable to bridge the abyss that divides them.

He asks nothing from her. For weeks nothing changes: not the canvas and the acrylic paint, the paper and the typewriter, nor the love he gives her. Why criticize? There is no hurry for her to get down to work. He only needs to believe – that is, hope – that she will take notice of his thoughtfulness. But she doesn't care. He expects some sort of excuse, a word to the effect: "You can't force inspiration," or "I'm letting my ideas settle." Nothing. What follows are tedious hours of waiting and anxiety while she locks herself inside. Inside the prison of things. He is coping and his heart skips a beat when he hears the door handle turn and sees her in the hallway collapse onto the marble floor.

When he comes back home one night, he does not expect to find her there. To his surprise, she has set the table for two. There is the sweet aroma of dinner in the apartment. She is standing behind the kitchen counter, smiling. She tells him to sit at the table and pour himself a glass of the wine he has kept aside for a special occasion. Of course, he says nothing, he's rather pleased. There is more of the same wine down in the cellar where this bottle comes from. Discreet, he does not comment on her new-found happiness. She sits down, serves herself a glass of the wine and offers a toast to her feeling much better. He brings his index finger to his lips to discourage her from talking too much. For a second or two he shuts his eyes and lets happiness overwhelm him. Maybe she is ready to admit her love for him.

A woman of few words, she is as wild as a bird. And so he hangs on to her actions: how her fingers gracefully push aside a stray lock of hair, or again the way they bring the cigarette to her lips. These are fingers he now imagines skilfully handling a painter's brush. (He has yet to see her paint.) She lets him savour her gestures. He believes he is the one who robs her of them, but it is she who offers him each of her gestures. Whatever binds this couple is nurtured by this misunderstanding.

He wants to tell her she should not hurt herself as she does. He knows, however, that he would lose her, for what brings one to the other is precisely this struggle. He tells her how they are similar to one another, but that she is the stronger one. He sees as acts of courage her refusal to be an artist and the way she surrenders herself to the ravages of night. He does not know who he prefers: the woman she is now or the image he created of the woman she once was.

She drinks the entire bottle of wine by herself. She laughs and says that if she is an artist it is thanks to her drinking. In both cases, she's worked wonders. "The reward's in the effort," she says. It's the unquenchable thirst in her that makes her drink or paint, not inspiration.

On normal days, she settles down into a routine allowing herself to be won over by order and things. That is when she gets ready to work. She places the typewriter on the table and slides a sheet of paper into the roller. Suddenly anxiety takes hold of her. She huddles up in a corner and bites her fingernails. She smokes one cigarette after another until the need for a drink becomes irrepressible. By the second glass, the nervousness is gone and she feels she has finally freed herself of the thing she hates most in the world: temperance.

Before meeting her, he was someone who was, day by day, losing whatever in life made him click. As though there was a minuscule hole in his feet through which time seeped out of his body. He was empty, except for this weariness from which he knew he could never totally free himself. Then she appeared. It was like Saul seeing the Light, the inexplicable and dazzling light that comes down and for a while seals the cracks within.

She never takes him for a lifepreserver. Contrary to what he might think, she too notices her boat filling up with water. It is his smile that seduces her. His is the sad smile of someone who can't be surprised anymore and who expects nothing from life. Yet he isn't a prey to bitterness. She walks up to him and compares his smile to the stars whose light has died long before their reflection reaches us.

As if he is giving her the time of day, he says: "I haven't made love to a woman in a long time." She laughs. They drink till sunrise. She takes his hand and asks if he'll give her a bed as gift. She undresses and slides under the covers. She points to the darkened veins on her arms: "This is how I come."

For the past days, the only time she has conversed with him is while she is fast asleep. He sits beside her and relentlessly watches over her: he doesn't want her to die on him. In a black book he scribbles the words she mumbles to him. He tells himself that she might need those notes one day. Between her bouts of delirium and respite, he invents a story in which he is a sad valiant knight or a prince charming whose kiss on the woman's chapped lips awakens her from the world of the dead. He has no idea that she is already dead, nor that he can be cut down by the blades between her legs. Or maybe he knows, but has agreed to offer himself in sacrifice to save her. And so, every time her body sinks in a sweat of distress, she asks for a fix. He carefully prepares the syringe which she injects into her arm. This is how he gives her pleasure.

He tells himself: Without love we are nothing. His eyes are wild and dazed by the euphoria the poison he serves her produces. He tries in vain to understand her story. He believes that to crack open the mystery that cloaks her will bring him closer to her. The truth is that he himself has embarked on the long journey within.

She speaks to him softly. Her voice is tinny, almost broken. She talks about a dream in which he was present. He is silently walking by her side. They come to a brook which they know they must cross. Obviously this is a sign. But she refuses to wet her feet. "The water is too cold," she says. He stretches over the brook, his face in the water, as she walks across the human bridge.

He asks if she is feeling better. She doesn't know. It has been so long since she's felt this way she can't tell if this is suffering, happiness, or something in between. He tells her: "I love dreams in which you give me a role to play, no matter how small."

It's her turn to smile now. She says she understands how love can be a virtue if it is not consummated. Behind the open door, he looks at her dressing. He shuts his eyes, drunk on the memory of her threatening perfection. Her body is a masterpiece. He quivers at the thought that, once dead, she could, with a single blow, extinguish the passion burning inside him.

She kisses him on the forehead. She rolls up her sleeves. He is surprised to see that her arm is free of needle marks. Had she been dreaming? Had she gone crazy and imagined him plunging the needle into her protruding vein? "I feel much better." He replies that he too is glad to see how her thin arm has healed. He tells her he finds the hollow of the arm one of the most sensual parts of the female body, how he would like to, just once, lower his lips there.

He begs her: "Walk all over me. Crush my body so that I may find my way. I'm naked and I offer you my nakedness. May it help you reach beyond this body from which I would very much like to free myself, but am forever bound. Walk all over me, my love. I want to forever carry in and on me the traces of your journey."

Their eyes, he tells himself, are roads of complicity that none can deny. It would be so easy for her to admit: "Yes, I love you." The fleeting thought brings him absolute grace. Let this be enough for the time being; this is all he needs to escape death.

Does her silence condemn him to death? He doesn't know and will never know. As always she leaves without a word. She is gone, as beautiful as the black sun on her dress. Will she come back? He doesn't know, will never know. Each day is made up of uncertainties that gnaw away at the foundations of his heart. He knows that a promise is not a contract for hope. Yet he is hopeful.

She comes back in the morning. It's the first time he has waited so long for her. Soon he looks at her and says she is the eulogy of wine and desire. His is a song of praise before disenchantment. He stares at her with eyes filled with questions. "Why are you so beautiful? What are you looking for?" "Nothing," she answers. "I want nothing, and contrary to what you think, nothingness is exactly what the order of things demands from us."

He searches for this nothingness he doesn't understand so that he may offer it to her, a nothingness that will pull her out of death and bring her back to herself. He knows, and does not doubt it one instant, that answers can be found in a spot that lies between surrendering to a nothingness that promises nothing and the nothingness that overflows with significance.

The hibiscus has been erect ever since the day she came to live with him. It is only now that he notices how the flower is blossoming gloriously. The flower waits for the perfect moment to burst open. This is the metaphor for their story. Like the hibiscus, he stands stronger. The pain that flows in his aging veins is about to disappear. He drinks a glass of water, and then another, and like the hibiscus grows taller. He smiles as the leaves darken under the raw morning light of the May sun.

She says, "Loving repels me. And it has nothing to do with you." What can he say but "I understand." Her smile is sadder than all the world sadness combined. She brushes her fingers on his cheek, knows he is lying. She would like to be able to fulfil his expectations and tell him how much she loves him, but this is something she cannot do. Were she to confess, he would not be able to forgive her.

She has met another man and tells him so over coffee in the morning. He doesn't know how to react. He wipes away a tear. "When are you leaving?" he asks. "I'm not going anywhere, unless you want me to." He tells her that this is her home, and walks away.

He doesn't come back home that night, or the night after. On the third morning, just as she is returning from her nightly escapades, she finds him on the marble floor in the hallway. At first she thinks of walking over his sleeping body, leaving it to its despair. But then compassion of sorts, which she knows little of, leads her to act differently. Cautiously, and in spite of her drunkenness and fatigue, she lies down beside the body of the man who loves her with a madness only love can afford. Such are her thoughts at this time.

She waits on the floor before she slowly and with some difficulty turns toward him. Her fingers unzip his fly and pull out his flabby member. Seconds later, the wilted flower regains its vitality. She lifts her skirt and pulls her underwear aside. She straddles him, not looking to satisfy herself. She allows herself to be entranced by the up and down motion, the ongoing rubbing. She lets out a moan, her body shaken by quick spasms that provoke a smile. A smile he would have cherished.

Every day is a silent requiem of departures. He convinces himself that each day is a death that brings him closer to a new dawn. There is nothing, except the nothingness she spoke about earlier, but which he has yet to find. Nothing can arrest the inevitable escape.

The steady tapping of the typewriter keys awakens him. He shoots to his feet and silently gambols to the kitchen. He has no intention of disturbing her. As he crosses the livingroom, he notices that she has moved the table in front of the window. He stops at the door and looks at her typing. Maybe she is unaware of his standing there, staring at her fingers hammering away. He flatters himself by believing he is the protagonist of her novel. Yes, he is its hero. He tiptoes to the kitchen, makes himself a cup of coffee, and writes his letter of resignation.

As far back as he recalls he has spent the greater part of his life re-inventing chaos. He believes that chaos – the chaos he and he alone creates – is responsible for life and rebirth. When she stumbled on to his path, he thought that she would sow seeds of trouble that would eventually grow into disorder. Stuck in the eye of the storm, all he can do now is to wait for the calm to set in, before he can gather the fleshy fruits that chance has scattered on this road to life, his destiny.

She spends her days typing away. Words rush out of her fingers, her childhood once so near is now so far. In the evening, instead of succumbing to fatigue, she goes out for a drink. She comes home early, usually before midnight, tipsy but never drunk. She'll never allow herself to stumble down the staircase again.

He wonders if she is still seeing the other man, but dares not ask her. The truth is, since she began writing her novel, they have rarely talked to one another. Certainly not since he found out what it is she is writing about. She says rather coldly: "No use prying. You can't read the manuscript before I finish it." This is when it occurs to him that she might be writing about him, their affair, a love story that never really begins.

One evening, while she is out, he bores a hole in the floor of his room, situated right above the dining room, so that he can spy on her working. He crouches down in his room, naked on the wooden floor. When his eyes grow tired, he lets his ears do the spying. He tries to decipher what words are being typed on the paper, but he falls asleep, entranced by the monotonous hammering on the keyboard. He makes out: "I've found love. I've found love, and now I must distance myself from it. If I don't, my passion for him will disappear as quickly as it appeared."

She almost forgets that he is there, thinks she lives alone. When she hears him walking down the stairs or in the hallway she tells herself that she should speak to him and inquire about how he is doing. But these altruistic bouts soon peter out. Her manuscript is moving along. This is all that matters for the time being. The world of words and the state of isolation these words induce do not quench her thirst. "I'll take a break tomorrow," she says, standing at the kitchen door. He lifts his weary eyes up to her. She adds: "Tonight I invite you to walk with me to the end of the night and stir up chaos in our lives."

They dress and go out like a normal couple, yet know there is nothing normal about them except this appearance of normalcy. He holds her and hopes to be able to rekindle the fire he used to have as a young man. This is all he cares about. There is laughter, large quantities of alcohol and music, and suddenly the second man materializes. Handsome, he is as bewitching as the calm before the storm. She introduces him to the other, kisses him on the cheek, and runs off with the second man, into the eye of the storm.

He knows there is nothing for him to do, now or ever. Never has so much grace befallen him, regardless of the fortune he has or the potions he could consume. He smiles a sad smile. The couple leaves. Later that evening, a young woman walks up to him and says she is a sinking boat desperately in need of a port for a while. He laughs at how fate works in strange ways. He invites the woman back to his house. As they make love, he realizes that his hands have turned into a vice tightening round the woman's fragile neck. He wants to put an end to the screaming.

He finds a note on the table: "Thanks for every-thing." The note was written by the stranger the night before. He is edgy, leaves it on the table so that his woman can notice that he too can go on without her. When she comes back, shortly after noon, he is sleeping on the sofa. She pours herself a drink, reads the note, and scribbles: "You're wel-come."

He boards up the window of his room in order to block out the sun. He rarely walks out of the room now, and when he does it is never for more than a few hours a day. His relationship to the outside world is reduced to the spy-hole in the floor where he listens and studies the woman at work. "In spite of myself I've become an accountant," he tells himself. "Not just a simple accountant, but an accountant of words. This is my real calling in life." In his madness, he calculates that she strikes the keyboard about twenty-five thousand times a day, which rounds off to about five thousand words or twenty pages of text. By his calculations, she has written a manuscript of eight hundred pages. He wonders what it is about him that pushes her to waste so much time and ink.

On certain evenings when she is out, he shaves and showers. He puts on his best clothes and walks to the bar where he first ran into her, where he hopes to run into her again. But he does not see her. Neither her, nor the second woman who once picked him up in such a peculiar manner. He drinks consciously, systematically, until he is piss drunk. He realizes that he is one lonely soul. Whenever he finds himself drunk to the point of no return, he picks up the first woman he meets and invites her back home. But soon rejects her by collapsing on his bed, dead drunk in the deep sleep of solitude.

She knocks on his bedroom door, pushes it open and says: "Come, I'll make you a strong coffee." He stumbles out of bed, his head cupped in his hands. Her smile is a command, she expects a reaction from him, a word or two. His response: "You're radiant. Is love doing this to you?" "I'm nearly finished the manuscript," she says. "You'll be able to read it soon." He feels better. The headache's gone. He tells himself, "This is where the story comes to an end." He believes that there is a calm before and after a storm, and that in between lies chaos, which gives birth to freedom.

He walks out of his refuge, for it is no longer necessary for him to spy on her. There is soon a change in climate; she punches in the final period to the story. The typing is not frenetic anymore. She spends most of the day reading the first draft, making a correction here, clarifying an idea there. At least this is what he likes to believe, slumped as he is on the bench on the veranda, smoking cigarette after cigarette, allowing his mind to digress from his worries. To be celebrated in a book – love will make him immortal.

All day long she drinks and revises her manuscript. Writing for so long has left her dry. The ink that poured out of her body needs to be replenished. She believes that truth can only come from within, from one's self. It is one's duty to allow it to burst forth and deliver its ghost.

The waiting. He believes that he spent all this for one sole purpose: to give birth to himself, to the couple. This gift of life they offer themselves, this fountain of perpetual movement one can only hope to ever drink from. Characters born of words and paper can only rise fully to their truth with the big bang of perfect fiction. There can only be equilibrium if equilibrium itself is on the verge of toppling over.

In the centre of the table lies the eight-hundred page manuscript like an imposing tombstone. The rest is tidy: the typewriter, the unused paper, the ashtrays. On the pile of paper, a note which invites him to read the story on order and things. Also scribbled is a sentence warning him that she will soon be back and hopes by then he will have read the work. He carries the enormous manuscript to his room and shuts the door. He hesitates before turning over the title page. When at last he does, the dedication smacks him on the face: "To the other, he who filled the space the first never did."

She gives herself totally to the other, not once thinking about the one who holds in his hands the fruit of several months' work. She is free, liberated, elated. She has, in one way or another, kept a promise she made to no one: to give herself life.

"I could no longer pretend. Yet I would have loved to have been able to offer him more than pity. Unfortunately, my stay with him was just that: pity. At one point I actually believed that sympathy, or perhaps solitude, would enable us to connect. Impossible. For that to have occurred it would have been necessary for us not only to have died but to have been reborn in chaos. And this would had to have happened in the same breath. Today, as I find myself about to be born anew, there is nothing left to do except offer him words that will fall on him like a death sentence. I'm afraid. This is the death of what never did exist between us."

Contrary to what she promised, he knows that she will never be coming back. Time too, he tells himself, no longer counts. He spends his days waiting for her, sitting on the bench on the verandah. He holds her manuscript close to his heart, and repeats the last paragraph of the book. He tries hard to find in those sentences some trace of hope that will keep his dreams alive. There is only the strong wind that tears down everything in its way. And so, less out of despair, for despair has abandoned him, than out of being tired of his servitude, he crumples the pages and throws them one by one at the foot of the curtains where he flips a burning cigarette. He walks up to his room and stretches out on the bed. He positions his hands over his belly and falls asleep, delighted by the idea that he will soon rise from his own ashes.

Stefan Psenak was born in 1969. Editor of Éditions L'Interligne (Ottawa) and the magazine *Liaison* from 1997 to 2003, he has published poetry, plays, short stories and a novel. In 1999, Psenak won the Trillium Award for the original French text of *On Order and Things* (*Du chaos et de l'ordre des choses*).

Printed in June 2003
at Gauvin Press Ltd.
Hull, Québec, Canada